Debt-Free Living: A Practical Guide for Individuals and Families

Table of Contents:

Introduction:

Welcome to "Debt-Free Living: A Practical Guide for Individuals and Families." In this book, we will embark on a journey to financial freedom, where you will learn how to liberate yourself from the shackles of debt and build a secure and prosperous future for yourself and your family.

Debt can be a significant burden, causing stress, anxiety, and limitations in your life. It's time to break free from this cycle and take control of your financial destiny. Whether you're struggling with credit card debt, student loans, or any other type of financial obligation, this book will provide you with actionable steps to become debt-free and stay that way.

We'll explore strategies for managing your money wisely, setting achievable financial goals, and making informed decisions about your finances. By the time you finish reading, you will have the knowledge and tools needed to transform your financial life and achieve lasting financial freedom.

Chapter 1: Understanding Debt

1.1 What Is Debt?

Before we dive into strategies for becoming debt-free, let's start by understanding what debt is. Debt is money that you owe to someone else. It can take various forms, such as credit card balances, loans, mortgages, and even unpaid bills. Debt typically comes with interest, which means you have to pay back more than you borrowed.

1.2 The Dangers of Debt

Debt can be a slippery slope that leads to financial stress, limited opportunities, and a reduced quality of life. It can hinder your ability to save for the future, make it challenging to cover unexpected expenses, and even strain your relationships. Recognizing the dangers of debt is the first step toward breaking free from its grip.

1.3 The Benefits of a Debt-Free Life

On the flip side, a debt-free life offers numerous benefits. You have more financial security, less stress, and the freedom to pursue your goals and dreams. You can save for retirement, invest in your children's education, and enjoy life without the constant burden of debt payments. Let's work together to make these benefits a reality for you and your family.

Chapter 2: Assessing Your Current Financial Situation

2.1 Creating a Budget

The foundation of any successful financial journey is a budget. A budget helps you track your income and expenses, giving you a clear picture of where your money is going. Start by listing your sources of income and then detail your monthly expenses, including necessities like rent or mortgage, utilities, groceries, and transportation.

2.2 Tracking Your Expenses

To gain a true understanding of your spending habits, track your expenses diligently for at least a month. This will reveal areas where you can cut back and save more money.

2.3 Identifying Debt

Identify all your debts, including the type of debt, the current balance, interest rates, and minimum monthly payments. This information will be crucial as you develop your debt repayment plan in Chapter 4.

Chapter 3: Setting Financial Goals

3.1 Short-Term and Long-Term Goals

Setting clear financial goals is essential for staying motivated on your debt-free journey. Short-term goals might include paying off a credit card or building an emergency fund, while long-term goals could involve buying a home or retiring comfortably.

3.2 Prioritizing Your Goals

Not all goals are equal. Some may take precedence over others based on your unique circumstances. Prioritize your goals to create a roadmap for your financial future.

3.3 Making SMART Goals

SMART goals are Specific, Measurable, Achievable, Relevant, and Time-bound. By making your goals SMART, you make them more attainable and easier to track progress.

Chapter 4: Creating a Debt Repayment Plan

4.1 The Debt Snowball Method

One popular debt repayment strategy is the debt snowball method, where you focus on paying off your smallest debts first while making minimum payments on larger debts. As you clear smaller debts, you gain momentum and motivation.

4.2 The Debt Avalanche Method

The debt avalanche method, on the other hand, prioritizes paying off debts with the highest interest rates first. This method can save you money in the long run but may take longer to see visible progress.

4.3 Negotiating with Creditors

Don't be afraid to negotiate with your creditors. Many are willing to work with you to establish more favorable repayment terms.

4.4 Debt Consolidation

If you have multiple high-interest debts, consider consolidating them into a lower-interest loan or a balance transfer credit card. This can make your debt more manageable and save you money on interest.

Chapter 5: Building an Emergency Fund

5.1 Why an Emergency Fund Is Crucial

An emergency fund acts as a financial safety net, protecting you from unexpected expenses like medical bills, car repairs, or job loss. It prevents you from relying on credit cards or loans during tough times.

5.2 How to Start an Emergency Fund

Begin by setting a goal for your emergency fund, such as saving three to six months' worth of living expenses. Start small if necessary, and gradually build it up over time.

5.3 Maintaining and Growing Your Fund

Once you've established your emergency fund, continue to contribute to it regularly. As your financial situation improves, consider increasing the size of your fund to provide even greater security.

Chapter 6: Reducing Expenses and Increasing Income

6.1 Cutting Unnecessary Costs

Identify areas where you can cut back on spending. This might include dining out less, canceling unused subscriptions, or finding more cost-effective ways to meet your needs.

6.2 Maximizing Your Income

Look for opportunities to increase your income. This could involve negotiating a raise at work, taking

on freelance projects, or exploring
new career paths.

6.3 Side Hustles and Additional Income Streams

Side hustles and part-time jobs can provide extra income to put toward debt repayment and savings. Consider your skills and interests when exploring these opportunities.

Chapter 7: Managing Credit Wisely

7.1 The Importance of a Good Credit Score

A good credit score is essential for obtaining favorable interest rates on loans and credit cards. Monitor your credit score regularly and take steps to improve it if necessary.

7.2 Responsible Credit Card Use

If you use credit cards, do so responsibly. Pay your balances in full each month to avoid high-interest charges, and only use credit for necessary expenses.

7.3 Avoiding Temptation and Impulse Buying

Practice self-discipline when it comes to spending. Avoid impulse purchases and only buy items that align with your financial goals.

Chapter 8: Avoiding Future Debt

8.1 Creating a Sustainable Budget

Your budget should be sustainable over the long term. It should allow you to live comfortably while also making progress on your financial goals.

8.2 Smart Financial Decision-Making

Think carefully before making major financial decisions, such as buying a home or car. Consider how these choices will impact your overall financial picture.

8.3 Saving and Investing for the Future

Once you've become debt-free, shift your focus to saving and investing for your future. This will help you build wealth and achieve your long-term financial goals.

Chapter 9: Staying Motivated

9.1 Celebrating Small Wins

Celebrate your achievements along the way, no matter how small they may seem. Recognizing your progress will keep you motivated.

9.2 Finding Support and Accountability

Share your goals with a trusted friend or family member who can provide support and hold you accountable. Consider joining a financial community or working with a financial advisor.

9.3 Visualizing Your Debt-Free Future

Imagine the life you'll lead when you're debt-free. Visualize your goals and the financial freedom you'll enjoy. This mental picture will inspire you to keep going.

Chapter 10: Living a Debt-Free Life

10.1 Enjoying the Benefits of Financial Freedom

As you become debt-free, you'll experience reduced stress, increased financial security, and the ability to pursue your dreams.

10.2 Teaching Financial Responsibility to Children

Pass on your financial knowledge and values to your children, setting them up for a successful financial future.

10.3 Giving Back and Building Wealth

Consider using your financial freedom to give back to your community and invest in your own future wealth.

Chapter 11: Common Pitfalls to Avoid

11.1 Falling Back into Debt

Stay vigilant and avoid repeating past mistakes. Stick to your budget and financial plan.

11.2 Overextending Yourself

Don't take on more debt than you can handle. Live within your means and resist the temptation to overspend.

11.3 Ignoring Financial Warning Signs

Pay attention to financial warning signs, such as mounting debt or dwindling savings. Address these issues promptly to avoid a crisis.

Chapter 12: Resources for Continued Learning

12.1 Recommended Books and Websites

Explore additional resources to continue improving your financial knowledge and skills.

12.2 Financial Advisors and Counseling Services

Consider seeking professional financial advice when needed. Financial advisors can provide tailored guidance for your unique situation.

Conclusion: Your Journey to Debt-Free Living

Congratulations on taking the first steps toward debt-free living. By following the principles and strategies outlined in this book, you have the tools to achieve financial freedom and secure a prosperous future for yourself and your family. Remember, the path to debt-free living may have challenges, but with determination and discipline, you can overcome them and enjoy the many benefits of a debt-free life. Good luck on your journey to financial success!